Listen To Him

COACH ROSCOE

authorHOUSE®

AuthorHouse™
1663 Liberty Drive
Bloomington, IN 47403
www.authorhouse.com
Phone: 833-262-8899

Published by AuthorHouse 07/28/2021

ISBN: 978-1-6655-3323-2 (sc)
ISBN: 978-1-6655-3322-5 (e)

Library of Congress Control Number: 2021915249

Print information available on the last page.

Any people depicted in stock imagery provided by Getty Images are models, and such images are being used for illustrative purposes only. Certain stock imagery © Getty Images.

This book is printed on acid-free paper.

Because of the dynamic nature of the Internet, any web addresses or links contained in this book may have changed since publication and may no longer be valid. The views expressed in this work are solely those of the author and do not necessarily reflect the views of the publisher, and the publisher hereby disclaims any responsibility for them.

Scripture quotations marked KJV are from the Holy Bible, King James Version (Authorized Version). First published in 1611. Quoted from the KJV Classic Reference Bible, Copyright © 1983 by The Zondervan Corporation.

CONTENTS

FOREWORD

A Wise Man Will Hear

To know wisdom and instruction; to perceive the words of understanding; To receive the instruction of wisdom, justice and judgement, and equity; To give subtility to the simple, to the young man knowledge and discretion. A wise man will hear and increase learning; and a man of understanding shall attain unto wise counsels: To understand a proverb, and the interpretation the words of the wise and their dark sayings...The fear of the Lord is the beginning of knowledge: but fools despise wisdom and instruction. My son hear the instruction of thy father and forsake not the law of thy mother for they shall be an ornament of grace unto thy head and chains about thy neck. -Proverbs 1:2-9 KJV

I had to step back. I had to close myself from this world; there is not much to love about this world. I set myself apart. I thought I almost lost my mind a few times, but it took me a few years to get back up. I really almost lost it all. I almost threw in the towel. I really had nowhere to turn. Could not tell anyone because there was no one to turn to. I felt like I was dumped on a desert. I had a phone no one I mean no one would or even if they wanted to could help me.

I was broken down so bad that if you saw me, you only saw a shell of me. But one day, I woke up and said "Hold up, who am I?" I checked my heart and it was beating. I checked my chest and air was filling my lungs. But something told me to check my heart again. Yet this time it was not just beating…it was talking to me. *Wait…wait…wait.* My spirit starting moving yet my body stayed still. Suddenly, I felt as if I gained muscle and became lighter.

Look around...is this a box? I started to speak, but there was no person to hear my response. Sometimes a conversation doesn't need a person there to be started. When a person listens to the Lord, He will talk to you in His time, not yours. *Move your arms...take a deep breath...get up...you are not dead.* I felt a power that I had never known.

When the voice of God speaks to you, you listen. You get up off your butt and do as a lion does and hunt. *I did not make you to quit....I MADE YOU TO WIN.* I thought I was washed up...

BUT GOD RESTORED ME

CHAPTER 1

The hunt is on.

I gave you a good chance to destroy me. I laid down but didn't die.

I was down, but not counted out.

I am not who I used to be. I am made new.

The only things that I am now are focused and happy.

I have none of that other stuff people have like sadness or fear.

I am not the same and I will only get stronger.

The stronger I get, the more trouble I will cause the devil.

CHAPTER 2

I will not let the Devil beat you or Myself. He already lost. Did you forget? I don't think you realize the Devil cannot harm you unless you let Him. Let me take a moment of silence….let us pray. Shhhhh…..he knows what is in my mind and heart. Amen. Is that your heartbeat? Or is it mine that reminds me to let God fight on my behalf.

I am on a rampage for The Lord. I will not stop because I love The Lord. DO YOU?

CHAPTER 3

You cannot change your past, but God can change you for your future. I do not look like I've been through the fire. I don't look or act like I have done a lot of sin, but I have. I thought I sinned so much that I could not be used by God. But God had to remind me he sent his only son to save our lives and wash away our sins with the Blood of Jesus. Thank you, Jesus, for dying on the cross for us. Yes, you can pray without ceasing. I have and so can you

In Psalms 119:15-19, it says: *I will meditate in thy precepts, and have respect unto thy ways. I will delight myself in thy statutes: I will not forget thy word. Deal bountifully with thy servant, that I may live, and keep thy word. Open thou mine eyes, that I may behold wonderous things out of thy law.* These words spoke volumes to me. It made me realize that I had to make a change within myself in order to be closer to Him and what He had in store for me. In 2009, things began to change. It was at that time how I started going back to church. 2009 was coming to an end and I was drowning fast and I mean fast. I didn't have anywhere to turn. There were things happening around me that I could not get explain, but I had to pray. Demons come out of Him or Her in the name of Jesus, Amen. Prayer changes things, if you don't believe me, try it. Have you prayed at least 1 time today?

We should always throughout the day thank God even when things are not going our way. God's got it under control. The Devil is never going to win. You may have knocked me down a few times, but you have not and cannot knock me out. I am built Lord Tough, not Ford Tough. I was built to last. The Devil thought I would quit, but I don't, and I won't with the lord on my side.

LET'S GO GOD!

CHAPTER 4

How many times do you talk to the Lord? He is always listening and always waiting for us to speak to Him. Do you give God the time He needs to talk to you? He should not always have to speak to us first. We should be the ones seeking Him. Every single one of us should have set goals we want to reach in order to better serve the Lord. My goals to serve God:

- Keep strong faith

- To continuously pray

- Protect and earn

- Help the Church grow

But, while these goals are for me to better serve God, I know that these goals also must stay out of His way. In doing all that I have set to do, these goals will allow me to stay spiritually lead by Him. Ask yourself: What are your goals?

CHAPTER 5

Men, do we lead by good example? Do we teach young men to be a man of God? God's power is **THE GREATEST POWER.** No one or anything comes before God You must remember to always, I mean always give God the glory He deserves. When you don't have anyone to teach you, God will. To lead by example, we must humble ourselves. I know that God sees everything that I am doing. God has set the ultimate example and we must strive to be that. Trust me, I know because He taught me. Young men and women do what they see. If you feel that you are not doing your best, ask God. He is the only one with the answer. Trust Him. If you doubt, you give the Devil a chance to take over. Never allow that to happen. When in doubt, you fill in these blanks and God will give you all the strength and encouragement you will ever need.

- *No weapon _____ against me shall _____.*

- *God is not a man that shall _____.*

- *Who do you serve? _____*

- *Do you trust _____?*

- *Do you love _____?*

- *_____ supplies my every _____.*

- *I pray to _____ every _____.*

- *God still _____ me.*

CHAPTER 6

ARE YOU PAYING ATTENTION?
DO YOU HAVE THE FAITH?

I do. Learn to listen to the Lord. He will answer you. He will provide for you. He loves you. His love for you knows no bounds. Love God and love yourself. God loves you all the time. Love is the only thing that can conquer hate. This world is full of it and if one is not careful, it can consume you. So many things tried to make me hate this world and tried to make me apart of it. But, with renewed faith and trust in God, I figured out that it is my duty to show the world just how much favor I have in His grace. Think for a moment and answer this question truthfully: Are you of this world or just in the world?

We must read the word of God. It is ok to set yourself apart from others sometimes. When you do, there will be times when some people won't understand why. But it is necessary for be able to grow and they shall see why do did so. This shows growth and shows others who you work for. I work for God and God alone. There will be people who come into your life who work for the devil and will try to pull you down by any costs. These same people will try to keep you from going to the Lord's House. If you don't want to go in church, that is the trick of the enemy. Trust God. God is everywhere, just look around you. Never doubt that he is there.

God does not lie. He will never lead you astray. All He asks of you is to believe in Him. He wants to hear from you. Take time to talk to the Lord. He will not judge you for talking to him. It does not matter where or when you talk to Him, just start talking. He talks to us all the time, but so many of us do not listen closely enough. Has God spoken to you yet? Will you listen if He speaks to you? Shhhhh, just listen.

CHAPTER 7

GOD really works in MYSTERIOUS ways. I know this by EXPERIENCE. There is a plan for your life that God has set. The Lord sends people in your life to help you be faithful to him. You must be faithful to Him before you can be faithful to others. When you are faithful in all of your actions, then God will revel and reveal to you limitless blessings. Always give GOD the glory, the honor, and the praise that He deserves. All victories are sweatless because Jesus already won the battle. God's plan for your life is to live better through Him. Are you willing to follow His plan for you? When you open your heart and your mind, God can speak to you. He speaks through songs and through His Word. Our minds and souls are like water. Water can be disrupted and troubled, just like we can be if we are not walking with God. Yet, when we are still like a beautiful lake, we can listen and hear everything that God is saying to us. You must guard your eyes, ears, and mind to those who want to lead you astray. When God calms your spirit, take heed. He is preparing you for battles that you have yet to see. Can you honestly say you are ready for war? You are not and cannot be defeated. Remember, Jesus already won the battle for you. Learn to depend only on God. Man cannot do the things God can do for you. When you decide to take this journey with God, remember these things. The Holy Spirit will never steer you wrong. Be a servant to God with all your soul. God speaks to us all, we just have to listen. Just as he spoke to Samuel in 1 Samuel 3:4, 7-10 KJV, you must listen.

The Lord called Samuel and he answered, Here am I... Now Samuel did not yet know the Lord, neither was the word of the Lord yet revealed unto him. And the Lord called Samuel again the third time, and he arose and went to Eli and said, Here am I, for thou didst call me. And Eli perceived that the Lord had called the child. Therefore, Eli said unto Samuel, Go lie down and it shall be, if he call thee, thou shalt say, Speak, Lord; for thy servant hearth. So, Samuel went and lay down in his place And the Lord came, and stood, and called as at other times, Samuel, Samuel. Then Samuel answered, Speak for thy servant heareth.

ARE YOU LISTENING YET?

IN JESUS' NAME, AMEN

Printed in the United States
by Baker & Taylor Publisher Services